Hide and Seek

NATURE'S BEST VANISHING ACTS

ANDREA HELMAN
PHOTOGRAPHS BY GAVRIEL JECAN

Walker & Company New York

This book is dedicated in loving memory to Adelle Helman: mother, mentor, friend—and one of nature's natural beauties. Forever in my heart.

With deepest appreciation to my father, Sam Helman (thank you, Mom), for filling my life with a love of music, words, and shameless curiosity.

Thank you to Greg Green for his generosity.
—A. H.

This book is for my son, Mahasamut Mateo, and my dear wife, Mallika. Without your support, understanding, and love, this book could not have been accomplished. Thank you.

Thank you to Art Wolfe Inc. for the support in getting some of these photographs.
—G. J.

First published in the United States of America in 2008 by
Walker Publishing Company, Inc.
Distributed to the trade by Holtzbrinck Publishers

For information about permission to reproduce selections from this book, write to Permissions, Walker & Company, 175 Fifth Avenue, New York, New York 10010

Library of Congress Cataloging-in-Publication Data
Helman, Andrea.
Hide and seek : nature's best vanishing acts / Andrea Helman ; photographs by Gavriel Jecan.
p.   cm.
ISBN-13: 978-0-8027-9690-5 • ISBN-10: 0-8027-9690-7 (hardcover)
ISBN-13: 978-0-8027-9691-2 • ISBN-10: 0-8027-9691-5 (library binding)
1. Camouflage (Biology)—Juvenile literature. I. Jecan, Gavriel, ill. II. Title.
QL759.H43 2008   591.47'2—dc22   2007024242

Book design by Michelle Gengaro-Kokmen

Visit Walker & Company's Web site at www.walkeryoungreaders.com

Printed in China
(hardcover) 10 9 8 7 6 5 4 3 2 1
(reinforced) 10 9 8 7 6 5 4 3 2 1

SAVANNA/GRASSLANDS

Rolling hills, grasses, wildflowers. Found all over the world, grasslands have different names depending on their location. Plains, prairies, steppes, pampas—all provide food and shelter for plants and animals as diverse as kangaroos and snakes. Savannas, open tropical grasslands, are scattered with trees and scrubs and cover almost half of Africa, supporting a spectacular variety of wildlife. A transition between forest and grassland, the majestic savanna has features of both.

PRONGHORN ANTELOPE

Swatches of brown, tan, and white. Grass, snow, rocks, and rumps. It's winter in Yellowstone National Park and the wandering herd of pronghorn antelope becomes part of the patchwork scene of the season. Pronghorns live on open plains and semideserts and can spot a moving object miles away. They are the fastest land mammals in the western hemisphere. If danger approaches, a pronghorn raises the white fur on its rump to warn the herd, leaping 20 feet in a single bound and cruising at 30 miles per hour. Like rubber soles, pads on its hooves help it travel quickly and quietly to escape from wolves, coyotes, and bobcats.

VERVET MONKEY

Bark! Bark! A leopard is near. *Cough! Cough!* Watch out for eagles. *Chutter! Chutter!* That snake will gobble you whole. Vervet monkeys warn the group of danger; each unique call identifies the predator, alerting family and friends. Focusing through the foliage in its savanna home, the stocky vervet blends in and looks out for trouble. Eating and sleeping in the trees, it ventures to the ground in search of insects or spiders to spice up a flower, fruit, and leaf lunch.

LEOPARD

A crisscross of branches and grasses, bright sunlight, and harsh dark shadows surround and hide the dramatic spotted coat worn by the most lethal and patient predator: the leopard. It waits. It sniffs the air. It listens. Slowly, silently, gracefully, it creeps within a few feet of an unsuspecting gazelle. *Womp!* One victorious pounce. A delicious prize. The successful hunter carries as much as three times its weight up, up, up, high out of its competitors' reach, where it can dine for days in the treetops.

GREVY'S ZEBRA

Dusk on the dusty African savanna. It's a risky time to drink, but the Grevy's zebras are on the alert. Lions and hyenas are out of sight but not out of mind. There is safety in numbers, so they gather together. Their dazzling black-and-white stripes make a dizzying scene, shimmering in the rising heat waves. The stripes seem to run together, making it difficult for a hungry predator to pick out just one zebra. When one does attack, an alarm call passes through the herd. Run! With bodies almost touching, they can go for hours, outrunning a lion. It's a dangerous life, but loyal zebras take care of each other every day in their fight for survival.

SEA

Earth, the "Watery Planet." All oceans flow into each other, covering 70 percent of Earth's surface—making it the largest environment. Its abundance, beauty, and variety of life-forms are unmatched. Trillions of plants and creatures—from the tiny sea sponge to the whopping whale, from fish to fungi—are interconnected, depending on each other for food and shelter. Wind, rain, and temperature on land are influenced by this immense, watery world.

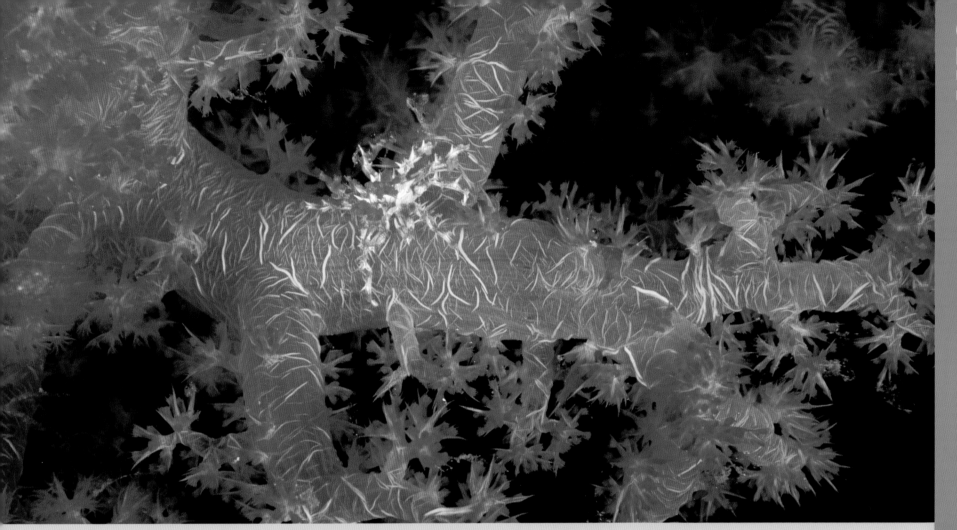

CANDY CRAB

Like a tree swaying in the wind, the soft coral moves with the water's currents, and the colorful candy crab hangs on and hides out. Holding tight to the coral tree, the creative crab nips off some polyps and sticks them on its back or pulls the branches around it to fool a predator. Eating the polyps transfers the red pigments to the crab, conveniently coloring it red . . . from the inside out!

MARINE IGUANA

Strong waves bombard the rugged, rocky shores of the Galápagos Islands. After a dive to feed on algae and seaweed, the primitive-looking marine iguana emerges from the cold Pacific waters to spend serious time warming its soot-colored body in the sun. The cold-blooded creature is the only lizard in the world that lives in marine water. Stretching out on the black lava rock, its black body tricks the Galápagos hawk, its keen-eyed predator.

RUDDY TURNSTONE

On the rocky Arctic tundra, the muted colors and patterns of the ruddy turnstone's breeding feathers help protect it from predatory gulls and Arctic falcons. Waddling this way and that, the short-legged forager is busy, busy, busy. Named for their color and habit of turning over pebbles, stones, and seaweed, ruddy turnstones are constantly on the move, pecking and chasing and looking for the next marvelous morsel. Home is by the sea on any continental coastline, but they always return to the high Arctic to breed.

SEA OTTER

Like a log lazily floating on the water, the gregarious sea otter lounges on its back in a bed of kelp, blending into its marine environment and hopefully tricking hungry orcas or sharp-eyed eagle predators. Placing a rock on its furry belly, it cracks open a tasty sea urchin. Lunchtime! It flips over for a quick wash and rubs its dense fur to keep it clean and waterproof. Other members of the raft, or group, call it for a game of tag. A quick somersault to warm up and it's ready to play. Ah, life is good!

Camels live in the desert and so do penguins . . . just different kinds of deserts. Found on all continents except Europe, deserts are either hot and dry or cold and dry. What they do have in common is less than 10 inches of rain per year and a harsh habitat. Plants and animals must store the precious water, and flower seeds sometimes stay buried for years while awaiting rain. Deserts may look deserted, but burrowing or hiding under rocks or behind vegetation, life continues struggling to survive.

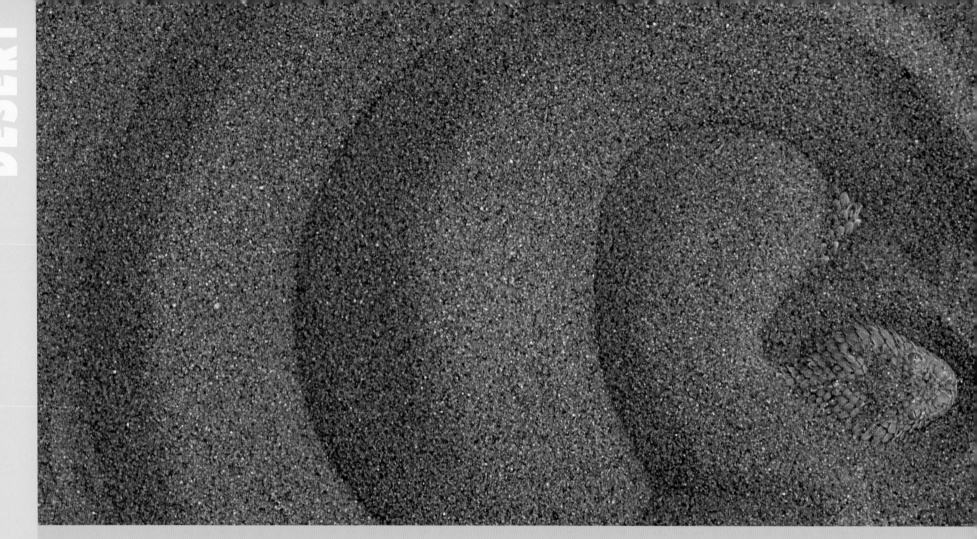

DESERT ADDER

Night is fading. The sun creeps over the horizon across the vast Namib Desert and the fog settles in. Slithering from side to side over the shifting sand, the small sidewinder coils up and licks the precious water droplets off its scaly body. When the sun comes up, the clever desert adder goes deep, deep down, burying itself into the sand. Only its eyes, perched on top of its heart-shaped head, and the tip of its tail are exposed. Its whole body feels the vibration of prey and its tongue collects their scent. It's keeping cool while hiding out, ready to ambush a passing desert lizard.

GREATER KUDU

The large, sensitive ears of the greater kudu perk up. The tall African antelope is on the alert, avoiding hyenas, lions, leopards, and wild dogs. In the Kalahari Desert, the greater kudu hides behind scrub brush. Its color is a perfect camouflage, whether it is sneaking away, frozen in place, or leaping over bushes up to 8 feet high to escape predators. The graceful horns are rarely used for fighting and grow to be 6 feet in length—as tall as a person.

AFRICAN GRASSHOPPER

Lying low and lounging around in full view, the tiny African grasshopper vanishes into the rocky sand. If staying perfectly still doesn't fool a predator, it uses its powerful back legs to jump away to safety. Grasshoppers are successful tricksters, resting on bark, branches, and leaves and staying out of danger while basking in the sun.

ARCTIC

Way up north, at the top of the globe, winter is a time of bone-chilling temperatures, blizzards, and constant darkness. It is so frigid, the land is permanently frozen beneath the surface, and for nearly six months the sun never comes up! But in the summer, the sun barely touches the horizon before it rises again. It is the "Land of the Midnight Sun." Layers of topsoil thaw, and more than 100 species of birds migrate to the Arctic tundra to feed. It is one of the world's coldest habitats; but for many living things—from plankton to polar bears, from wolves to whales—it is their home.

EURASIAN GOLDEN PLOVER

Hidden in the moss, lichens, and heather, the fluffy feathers of the Eurasian golden plover chick are colored to perfectly match its cozy Iceland habitat, hiding it from predatory gulls, falcons, and hawks. Mom is off scoring lunch. She runs-stops-pecks, hunting visually, even by moonlight. "Tloo!" The bulky bird will announce its presence long before you see it. When winter arrives, their food is frozen or covered by snow, so plovers migrate to new homes in western and southern Europe.

HARP SEAL PUP

Wedged in its snowdrift cave, a furry harp seal pup stays warm, blending into its white Arctic environment. It is hiding from hungry polar bears and waiting for Mom to return from feeding; but in just 12 days she will abandon it. Soon, its furry "white coat" will change to a "ragged jacket" as its thick fur molts and is replaced by a sleek, shiny, silvery gray pelt—all the better to vanish within its gray, watery home. It has many enemies and must learn to survive and protect itself from sharks, orcas, and bears.

ARCTIC

GRAY WOLF

A steely eyed gray wolf sniffs the cold Canadian air. Its keen sense of smell is 100 times more sensitive than yours. It's built for hunting big game, but for now, in the sunlight and shadows, its mottled coat of grizzly gray, brown, tan, and white is an effective camouflage between hunts. Living in family groups called packs, wolves travel, feed, and hunt together. As a team, they prey on weak and old deer, elk, antelope, and moose, feeding themselves and leaving leftovers for others. Eat or be eaten—it's the natural balancing act in the natural world.

FOREST

Below the canopy—the tip-top—of this peaceful place, the forest is a bustling habitat bursting with life. There are several kinds of forests on Earth—tropical, temperate, and boreal—which are all home to many animals, birds, insects, flowers, and vegetation. Forests provide food and shelter for their inhabitants and oxygen for us all. Tropical rain forests, warm and wet, have the richest variety of plant and wildlife on Earth. New species are discovered each year, along with valuable medicines for people. Saving the forests helps animals, plants, and humans.

FOREST

THREE-TOED SLOTH

Belly up! Slowly, slowly, the sloth sways through the tree branches, hanging around and living upside down. Even its coat falls from its belly . . . to its back. Three curved claws grasp onto the same tree for days at a time. Up in the treetops it avoids predators, blending in to the leaves with a greenish glow from tiny green algae that grow in the grooves of its long, shaggy hair. It's the perfect camouflage color in its Panamanian rain-forest home.

BENGAL TIGER

Big and bold, the Bengal tiger boasts beautiful black stripes against tawny orange fur. But in the light and shadow of the tall grasses, forests, and mangrove swamps of India, the outline of the powerful predator disappears. It's hiding. It's seeking. The biggest of all the big cats, the hungry Bengal tiger is nocturnal, hunting at night, killing the equivalent of 30 buffalo a year! It has the largest teeth of all the meat-eating animals and takes down prey two or three times its size with a lethal canine crunch.

MARBLED TREE FROG

Sticky fingers and sticky toes make the agile little tree frog an amazing climbing, jumping, and leaping machine, able to bound 40 times its length! But when the marbled tree frog wants to hide, it just hunkers down and hangs out on dried leaves or tree bark, disappearing into the patterns of the Peruvian rain forest, waiting for dinner to arrive. It's a "sit and wait" predator. Patient tree frogs use their large rotating eyes, sense of smell, and the vibrations of a passing creature to score a tasty meal of bugs, beetles, and ants.

CRYPTIC KATYDID

Hiding in plain sight, cryptic katydids fake out predators by mimicking, or imitating, the green leaves they love to eat. Their ears, tiny slits on their front legs, listen for their enemies: bats, birds, spiders, and tree frogs. When the katydid wants to communicate, it rubs its wings together and sings out in the night, "Katy did! Katy didn't! Katy did!" to attract a mate and to tell rivals, "Back off!"

MOUNTAINS

Spectacular sights, mountains are found on all the world's continents. Climb a mountain, and you'll pass through changes in vegetation, temperature, and wildlife. The top is treeless, the bottom generally covered by forest. Some mountains stand alone, but usually they're found in groups called chains or ranges. At the top, it's cold, snowy, and windy. Hardy plants hug the ground, golden eagles patrol, and sure-footed, warm-blooded animals adapt to the high life.

OWL BUTTERFLY

In the cool dawn and dusk hours, in the rain forest of the Peruvian Andes mountains, the owl butterfly busily forages for fruit. With just the flick of a wing, it changes from potential prey to potential predator. Are those owl eyes? Little birds love a lunch of butterflies, and owls love a lunch of little birds. Quickly, this large butterfly mimics the owl face the bird fears. Fooled again by fake eyes! Eyespots are effective fakery, and animals believe what they see in their struggle to survive each day.

PRAYING MANTIS

Look out! Its legs are tucked as if in prayer, but it's *prey* it's after. And the mantis is dressed for success: a mirror image of the twig it's imitating. With a vicelike grip, it quickly snatches an unsuspecting insect, a lizard, or even another mantis, with special spine-covered forelegs. *Chomp! Gulp!* It eats its prey live. A most effective hunter, this tiny terror lives in the highlands of Papua New Guinea, but its 2,300 relatives live in warm areas all over the world.

ELLIOT'S CHAMELEON

Motionless, the colorful and crafty chameleon stays still, disappearing into tree bark in the Rwanda mountains. Its bulging eyes rotate in different directions, searching the turf for tasty treats. Aha! It focuses both eyes to judge the distance and position of an insect. *Zap!* The sticky-tipped tongue shoots out at 20 feet per second. Success! Chameleons are nature's quick-change artists, exchanging one color for another to protect themselves from predators and become invisible to prey.

WHITE-TAILED JACKRABBIT

Standing up on strong hind legs, peeking about for danger, the white-tailed jackrabbit has eyes that see in a near-complete circle. Its long, buff-gray ears are barely visible in the tall grass of the Sierra Nevada Mountains. Ever alert, the rabbit can hear the faintest of sounds—a handy skill because its life is full of predators: foxes, coyotes, bobcats, cougars, snakes, owls, and eagles. Fluffy fur that matches the environment, speed, and keen eyesight also help the bounding bunny. To escape an enemy, jackrabbits can dash in a zigzagging pattern up to 50 miles per hour, leap 5 feet up in the air, or even swim to survive another day.

THE BACK STORY

(locations indicate where the photographs were taken)

GIRAFFE
Masai G.c. tippelskirchi
Tarangire National Park, Tanzania

Dotted across the vast, tan Tanzania savanna, dotted giraffes gracefully graze. Each coat pattern is unique and varies from region to region, camouflaging the giraffe in the harsh sunlight and leafy shadows against the tree-studded buff background. Hungry herbivores, they are always on the move, sleep just 30 minutes a day, and stand as tall as three men—making them great lookout towers! If a lion, leopard, or hyena approaches, heavy hooves or a swing of the head are powerful weapons.

PRONGHORN ANTELOPE
Antilocapra americana
Yellowstone National Park, Montana, U.S.A.

Although true antelope live in Asia and Africa, pronghorns are found only in North America. They get their name from the prong on each horn, which they shed every year at the end of breeding season. Living on grasses, cacti, and weeds, small scattered herds roam about in summer, expanding to 100 or more during winter. They often give birth to twins each year; just two days later, the babies can outrun a person.

VERVET MONKEY
Cercopithecus pygerythrus
Samburu Reserve, Kenya

Vervet monkeys live in complex, stable social groups of 10 to 50 individuals. Some female relatives form relationships that last a lifetime. Young vervets love to play—wrestling, tumbling, and pushing each other off a high perch! Females often stay with their mothers all their lives, but males leave at age five. Monkeys spend several hours each day grooming, removing dirt and parasites from one another's fur.

LEOPARD
Panthera pardus
Krueger National Park, South Africa

Seldom seen outside of protected game preserves, leopards are secretive, solitary cats that are equally at home in deserts, forests, or plains—wherever there is dense vegetation. Fast runners, good climbers, and strong swimmers, they are among nature's most efficient hunters. Leopard cubs have many enemies, so watchful, affectionate single mothers will hiss if danger is near. That means "Freeze! Don't move."

GREVY'S ZEBRA
Equus grevyi
Masai Mara National Reserve, Kenya

Grevy's zebra, an endangered species, is the largest of all the zebras. Many hours are spent grazing beside giraffes, wildebeests, and gnus. Zebras are actually white with black stripes, and they recognize one another by their pattern and cry. They can survive for days without eating or drinking, further protected from predators by their rotating eyes and keen sense of smell.

ESTUARINE STONEFISH
Synanceia horrida
New Britain, Papua New Guinea

The stonefish is the most venomous fish in the world, and it is almost impossible to see. Flaps of skin look like seaweed, and its knobby body matches its rocky coral home on the coastal reefs. For further disguise, it piles sand around its rugged body, opens its large mouth, and then lies motionless. *Womp!* With lightning speed, dinner is served.

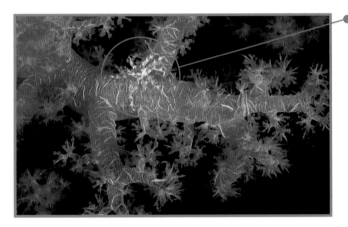

CANDY CRAB
Hoplophrys oatesii
New Britain, Papua New Guinea

Pink and white lines camouflage the candy crab. When it sheds its hard shell, it must protect its soft body from predators until the new case hardens. All crabs have five pairs of jointed legs; the way the joints are hinged makes the crab walk sideways. To escape an enemy, it contracts a muscle. *Poof!* It sheds a limb, which eventually grows back.

MARINE IGUANA
Amblyrhynchus cristatus
Galápagos, Ecuador

Sharp claws keep the lizard steady against strong waves and help it climb on and cling to the lava rocks. At night, marine iguanas sleep in huddles, and during the day they absorb heat through the black rocks. Because they feed on marine algae, their diet is full of salt. Do you see the white on their faces? That's salt! It is deposited in their nostrils and they have to—*ah-choo!*—sneeze it out.

RUDDY TURNSTONE
Arenaria Interpres
Glacier Bay, Alaska, U.S.A.

The ruddy turnstone uses its powerful neck muscles, strong legs, and upturned bill to turn stones and flip seaweed, earning the nickname "Seaweed Bird." Sometimes, several birds will join forces to overturn something heavy, like a fish. Digging holes in the sand, often larger than their bodies, they search for crusty crustaceans.

SEA OTTER
Enhydra lutris
Glacier Bay, Alaska, U.S.A.

No mammal, other than man, uses tools more frequently than the world's smallest marine mammal, the sea otter. Dense, waterproof fur, webbed feet, a rudderlike tail, and retractable claws keep it dry and help it navigate and catch food as it dives to the ocean floor for crabs, mussels, scallops, and snails. Sea otters love to play, but when it is time to rest or sleep, they will tether up to a forest of kelp.

DESERT

GILA MONSTER
Heloderma suspectum
Sonoran Desert, Arizona, U.S.A.

At twilight the colorful Gila monster emerges from its burrow, drags its bumpy, heavy body across the sand and pebbles of the Arizona desert, and disappears into its textured environment. One of only two poisonous lizards in the world, it chews venom into its victim through grooved teeth. The largest lizards in the United States, Gila monsters are rarely seen aboveground. They store fat in their bodies and tails, so three or four large meals will tide them over for a year.

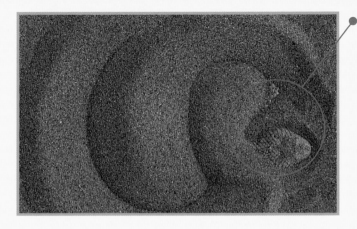

DESERT ADDER
Bitis peringueyi
Namib Desert, Namibia

Parallel grooves, amazingly left by the tiny desert adder, decorate the sand of the great Namib Desert. Also called a sidewinder, the 10-inch snake moves quickly in the harsh, windy environment. Throwing itself from side to side, right to left, only two spots of its body touch the hot sand at a time. Eventually its scales wear out, so the snake sheds its old skin up to four times a year.

GREATER KUDU
Tragelaphus strepsiceros
Kalahari Desert, South Africa

With stripes and spots and spectacular horns that spiral two-and-a-half times around, the greater kudu is one of the largest African antelopes. These adaptable animals are one of the few large mammals that can also thrive in areas of scrub woodland, abandoned fields, and pastures. Kudu eat many kinds of leaves, herbs, fruit, and tubers in the cooler hours of the day. They are peaceful and rarely aggressive, but if threatened, they make a loud call to alert the herd then bolt for cover, often stopping to look back—not always the safest move!

AFRICAN GRASSHOPPER
Parepistaurus
Samburu Reserve, Kenya

Found all over the world except in polar areas, grasshoppers are related to katydids and crickets, chirping like a cricket to establish their territory or attract a mate. With 10,000 species, grasshoppers come in many shapes, sizes, and colors, but they all seek to hop away or hide from such predators as birds, lizards, and other insects. The tiny African grasshopper has powerful jaws and sharp teeth to easily crunch lunch.

POLAR BEAR
Ursus maritimus
Manitoba, Canada

Polar bears are the biggest carnivores in the world, so they have no need to hide. But to seek, the sea bear's thick, waterproof coat is an effective camouflage. Quietly, it pads across its frozen Arctic homeland or imitates a chunk of floating ice, gliding slowly up to an unsuspecting meal of seal. To completely vanish in its white habitat, the polar bear places a huge paw over its black nose. Voilà!

EURASIAN GOLDEN PLOVER
Pluvialis apricaria
Vestur-Skaftafells, Iceland

When the Eurasian golden plover arrives in March, Icelanders consider this the beginning of spring. Gulls, falcons, and hawks—the plovers' enemies—watch for them too. A wary and alert bird, the Eurasian golden plover is splendid in its breeding plumage of gold and black. But in winter, it loses those dramatic colors and migrates to Europe, with some groups reaching as far as North Africa. Forming large flocks, they fly in tight formations that have been observed turning, twisting, and diving in unison high in the British skies.

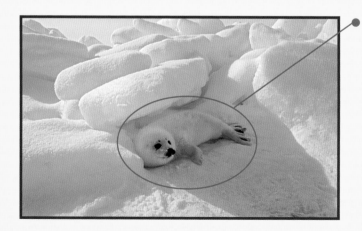

HARP SEAL PUP
Phoca groenlandicus
Isles de Madeleine, Canada

There is nothing like mother's milk. Human milk is 4 percent fat, but harp seal milk is 50 percent fat! The extra fat keeps the baby warm in the frigid Arctic temperatures. After its mom leaves, a baby seal must learn to swim on its own. At various life stages, it will eat different sea creatures. Living on both land and sea, the first year of survival is the hardest.

GRAY WOLF
Canis lupus
Yellowknife, Canada

Other than humans, wolves cover the broadest territory of Earth's mammals—from forests and plains to deserts and mountains. Long legs and large paws equipped with strong claws help them travel far and fast to feed, sometimes chasing a potential meal for up to 20 minutes. With a powerful bite, gray wolves are known to chomp down and hang on to their prey.

RUFESCENT TIGER-HERON
Tigrisoma lineatum
Llano, Venezuela

Patience and its brownish gray color make the tiger-heron a successful hunter. Standing perfectly still near a riverbank, it blends into the forested undergrowth. With lightning-quick reflexes, it spears a fish with a thrust of its long, pointed bill. Herons are crepuscular, meaning they're most active at dawn and dusk. When nesting, herons sit still and silent, head hunched down to blend in safely; if danger is detected, they stretch out their neck and fly away.

THREE-TOED SLOTH
Bradypus variegates
Bocas del Torro Islands, Panama

Everything about the sloth is slow: it even takes a month to digest a batch of leaves! It feeds anytime, but it can spend hours in search of a meal because it is very selective about which leaves will do. Green is a good color to be in the rain forest, but in the dry weather, sloths become brownish, to match the dying vegetation.

BENGAL TIGER
Panthera tigris tigris
Madhya Pradesh, India

In India, a land of many religions, tigers are often a symbol of strength. At 600 pounds, a tiger can roar loud enough to be heard up to 2 miles away. It is fearless, attacking an elephant or a rhinoceros, but if it loses its teeth to injury or old age, it will starve to death. Tigers don't like the heat, so they cool off in pools of water, where even this most powerful predator can become prey to a hungry crocodile.

MARBLED TREE FROG
Hyla marmorata
Madre de Dios, Peru

On all the world's continents except Antarctica, new species of frogs and toads are discovered every year—5,300 and counting—with the greatest variety found in tropical rain forests. Tree frogs come in many patterns and colors and are adaptable to water, land, and trees. They slowly change color, blending into their surroundings, disguising themselves to predator and prey, hiding by day and noshing by night.

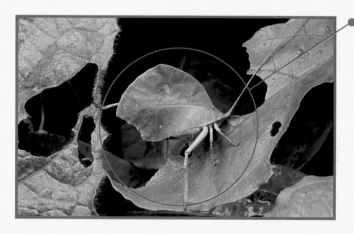

CRYPTIC KATYDID
Tettigonidae
Napo River, Peru

In the natural world, clever creatures will imitate, or mimic, others to stay alive. Leaves are the most commonly imitated. The cryptic katydid lunches on leaves and mimics the parasitic fungi of an imperfect leaf down to the veins, even adding a rip or two to complete the convincing disguise. Species of katydid are found on every continent but Antarctica.

ALPINE IBEX
Capra ibex
Alps, France

The sure-footed Alpine ibex, a wild goat, climbs the steep cliffs and hills of the French Alps, using altitude and its muted brown-gray coat to blend into its rocky environment as protection from predators. If threatened, it will use its impressive ridged horns to defend itself against wolves, bears, foxes, jackals, or lynx. Even a young kid learns that its horns are a good defense when cornered.

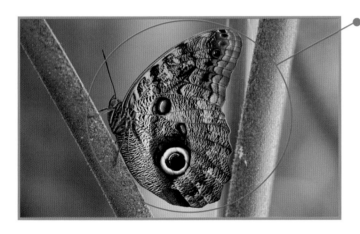

OWL BUTTERFLY
Caligo memnon
Manu National Park, Peru

Owl butterflies live only in Central or South America and use their eyespots and unique coloration for survival, avoiding the heat by spending the day safely perched on a tree trunk. Eyespots increase the survival of many creatures: beetles, fish, frogs, moths, and butterflies. Sometimes the eyespots help mimic the appearance of another critter, or they startle or lure a predator to attack an unnecessary body part, allowing the animal to escape.

PRAYING MANTIS
Mantidae
Highlands, Papua New Guinea

Although the praying mantis can walk, leap, and fly, camouflage is its best defense. An ambush hunter, it matches the color of its environment in shades of green, tan, and brown. A large mantis can cleverly catch a frog or even a mouse. After eating, it grooms itself much like a cat does. It's important to keep those antennae and huge, bulging, rotating eyes clean—all the better to find more food.

ELLIOT'S CHAMELEON
Chamaeleo ellioti
Virunga, Rwanda

The first chameleon lived on Earth 200 million years ago. Now there are 150 species. Chameleons automatically match their environment. Black, red, and yellow cells in their skin change color, depending on weather, light, and mood. Fused toes and a long, long tail keep chameleons balanced on branches and make them built for life in the trees.

WHITE-TAILED JACKRABBIT
Lepus townsendii
Sierra Nevada Mountains, California, U.S.A.

The fastest of all the rabbits and hares in the world, bounding up to 20 feet, the white-tailed jackrabbit will sometimes just lie still and low to the ground when threatened. But if caught or injured, it will scream! Jackrabbits are strict vegetarians, feeding at night on a variety of grasses, herbs, and shrubs. During the day, they rest in shaded, shallow, dug-out areas aboveground, which are scattered throughout their home range—some used generation after generation.

PHOTOGRAPHER'S NOTE

I'm so very fortunate to do what I love: travel and photograph what I see. I travel for about eight months out of the year, and my work takes me from deserts to tropical rain forests, from rocky coasts to remote mountain ranges. It is my mission to capture images that reflect the diversity of the natural world and inspire future generations to preserve it. —Gavriel Jecan